THE TITANIC
Lost Words

SENAN MALONY

KEY TO IMPORTANT ARTICLES

Look out for the following symbols through this book, highlighting key articles from the past.

FILM EXCERPT
Primary source material taken from a film about the subject matter.

SONG EXCERPT
Lyrics extracted from songs about the subject matter.

OFFICIAL SPEECH
Transcribed words from official government speeches.

GOVERNMENT DOCUMENT
Text extracted from an official government document..

LETTER
Text taken from a letter written by a participant in the events.

PLAQUE/INSCRIPTION
Text taken from plaques/monuments erected to remember momentous events described in this book.

INTERVIEW/BOOK EXTRACT
Text from an interview/book by somebody there at the time.

NEWSPAPER ARTICLE
Extracts taken from newspapers of the period.

TELEGRAM
Text taken from a telegram sent to or by a participant in the events.

An Hachette UK Company
www.hachette.co.uk

First published in Great Britain in 2005 by TickTock, a division of Octopus Publishing Group Ltd,
Endeavour House, 189 Shaftesbury Avenue, London, WC2H 8JY.
www.octopusbooks.co.uk

ISBN 978 1 84898 693 0

A CIP catalogue record for this book is available from the British Library

Printed in Hong Kong
10 9 8 7 6 5 4

Every effort has been made to trace the copyright holders, and we apologize in advance for any unintentional omissions. We would be pleased to insert the appropriate acknowledgments in any subsequent edition of this publication.

CONTENTS

INTRODUCTION

Above The Titanic never reached her destination of New York, sinking 1,000 miles due east of Boston, Massachusetts, and 375 miles southeast of St. John's, Newfoundland.

Below Titanic's makers White Star Line circulated lavish brochures to promote their great liners.

When the Titanic set sail on its maiden voyage in 1912, this true giant of a ship was the pride of a nation. It was the most luxurious liner in the world and was said to be the safest vessel ever built. But when it blundered into an iceberg in the near mid-Atlantic, the Titanic become the most famous shipwreck in history. It seemed impossible to imagine that one of the largest ships ever built could fail to reach its destination, but far out to sea, with the nearest point of land in any direction eight hundred miles away, the Titanic sank beneath the waves. Almost 1,500 of the people on board lost their lives in the tragedy.

In 1907, officials at the White Star Line shipping company put forward the idea of building the world's finest superships, bigger, safer and more luxurious than anything else on the water.

The first of these, the *Olympic,* was launched almost a year before her sister ship, the *Titanic.* The two ships were the biggest moving objects ever built, and an article written when the *Titanic* was under construction claimed it was "practically unsinkable". Yet when it hit the iceberg on the night of April 14, 1912, it did sink. The lives lost represented a waste of talent on a massive scale. Only 712 people escaped, fewer than a third of those aboard.

Centre *A rescue ring from the Titanic. The inscription signifies that the ship was registered in the port of Liverpool.*

In some ways the ship was unfortunate. The iceberg that sank the 269-metre superliner was not white, like most bergs, but black because it had recently capsized. The *Titanic* was also travelling at its fastest speed when it sailed into danger. Other contributing factors, however, could have been avoided. The *Titanic* had 2,201 passengers and crew aboard but lifeboat spaces for just 1,200. Despite the long time before the *Titanic* went down, nearly 500 lifeboat places were not filled. Official Inquiries were set up on both sides of the Atlantic to try to find a reason for the tragedy. Although the captain of the *Titanic* and half its officers died in the sinking, public opinion still wanted someone to be held accountable. Many people blamed the disaster on reckless navigation, while others pointed to the woeful lack of lifeboats. The inquiries held after the tragedy absolved most of the crew from responsibility, but also

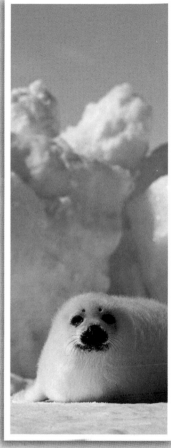

Above *Despite the fact that the Titanic was sailing straight into an area of the Atlantic riddled with icebergs, the crew seemed unconcerned.*

Below *A ticket to see the launch of the Titanic at Belfast. The ship was a huge draw, attracting thousands of spectators.*

Launch
OF
White Star Royal Mail Triple-Screw Steamer
"TITANIC"
At BELFAST,
Wednesday, 31st May, 1911, at 12-15 p.m.
Admit Bearer.

Above *Postcards marking the launch of the amazing steamer were hugely popular. This one was sent from the UK to Germany.*

came to many wrong conclusions that were believed for many years afterwards. There was, for example, the belief that the ship did not break in two when it sank, as many witnesses testified. This was accepted as fact until the discovery of the wreckage of the ship in the 1980s proved otherwise. The Inquiries did, however, lead to some valuable changes in maritime law. A host of safety reforms were brought in, and continue today, including the provision of lifeboats for all on board every ship. A new body, the International Ice Patrol, was set up to try to avert similar disasters.

Almost from the moment the *Titanic* sank beneath the icy water, efforts were devised to locate the wreck. Many of these schemes were bizarre, including a plan to locate the boat using electromagnets. The site of the *Titanic* remained elusive, and it was not until the development of electronic detection equipment in the 1980s that the search was successful. The remains of the liner were finally discovered by Dr. Robert Ballard and Jean Louis Michel on September 1, 1985. Since then, a company that was awarded salvor-in-possession rights, RMS Titanic, Inc. has conducted seven research and recovery expeditions to the wreck site. It has recovered more than 5,500 objects, ranging from personal possessions to a large part of the ship's mighty steel hull. Today, scientists are presented with a huge problem over what to do with the wreck

Below *A model of the Titanic showing how the ship looks now. Recent engineering evidence suggests that the unsinkable ship experienced a hull failure at the surface and broke into pieces before it went down.*

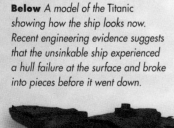

of the ship. Some people are calling for the *Titanic* to be raised from the ocean, conscious of the fact that the ship is decaying rapidly and is likely to break up completely in the near future. Others, however, feel that this would be simply inappropriate for what is essentially a mass grave, and that the remains should be left alone. What seems certain is that the public will continue to be fascinated by the tragic story of this great ship. This appetite for the story has been demonstrated by the success of numerous books and films about the disaster. The most recent of these is James Cameron's 1997 movie *Titanic*, starring Leonardo DiCaprio and Kate Winslet, which became the biggest grossing film of all time soon after it was released.

1. NEVER AN ABSOLUTION 2. DISTANT MEMORIES 3. SOUTHAMPTON 4. ROSE
5. LEAVING PORT 6. "TAKE HER TO SEA, MR. MURDOCH" 7. "HARD TO STARBOARD"
8. UNABLE TO STAY, UNWILLING TO LEAVE 9. THE SINKING 10. DEATH OF TITANIC
11. A PROMISE KEPT 12. A LIFE SO CHANGED 13. AN OCEAN OF MEMORIES
14. MY HEART WILL GO ON (LOVE THEME FROM 'TITANIC') PERFORMED BY CELINE DION
15. HYMN TO THE SEA

ALBUM PRODUCED BY JAMES HORNER

Above Titanic *merchandise, including spin-offs from the 1997 film, have sold millions across the world.*

Left Kate Winslet and Leonardo DiCaprio played the fictional sweethearts Jack and Rose, against the setting of the real wreck of the Titanic.

Above A First Class passenger ticket for the Titanic's maiden cruise.

Above Postcard of Olympic at New York after collision with the Hawke in September 1911.

The Royal Mail Steamer (RMS) Titanic was the second of a trio of gigantic liners commissioned by the White Star Line, one of the foremost steamship companies of the early 20th Century. The three ships were intended to give White Star Line control of the transatlantic market, taking people from Britain and Europe to the United States. They would be magnificent, of unparalleled size and the last word in luxury.

TITANIC'S OWNERS

The White Star Line began life operating emigrant vessels during the great Australian gold rush. When this ran out of steam, the company ran into financial difficulties, and in 1867 it was bought by Thomas Henry Ismay. Under the new ownership, the White Star Line commissioned ships from their partners, the Belfast shipbuilders Harland & Wolff. In 1870, the first ship was produced under this arrangement – *Oceanic*. It was the world's first superliner, and was followed by three sister ships of similar size. In 1891, Thomas Ismay's son, Joseph Bruce Ismay, was appointed President of the White Star Line and the company decided to focus exclusively on luxury liners. In 1902, the firm was bought by the American International Mercantile Marine Company, and two years later, Bruce Ismay became President of the company. In 1907, Ismay put forward plans to build two great luxury liners on a scale never seen before, with a third to follow if this direction proved successful. The emphasis was to be on luxury rather than speed, as the Belfast shipyard did not have the technology to compete with White Star's rival Cunard, and their ships, *Lusitania* and *Mauretania*. White Star's first two 'floating hotels' were to be known as *Olympic* and *Titanic*. A giant gantry – the world's largest – was constructed in Belfast to house the two vessels, each weighing 45,000 tons.

CLASS SYSTEM

It took three million rivets to hold together the thousands of inch-thick steel plates that made up the *Titanic's* hull. But it was the internal

BRILLIANT SCENE at QUEEN'S ISLAND

The vessel launched yesterday from the yard of Harland and Wolff deserves well her name *Titanic*, for none other would more aptly apply. The day was observed as a holiday by all who could leave work, some of these people joining the many of the leisured class who travelled long distances in order to witness the launch... On the river were many craft from small to large, and these were full to overflowing with sightseers. Five minutes before the appointed time there boomed out a double rocket, that being the signal that all was clear. Once more the whistle rang out, then the signal rockets boomed, the mountain of metal commenced to move, and there burst forth from the throats of the thousands of men, women, and children that were assembled at the yard, from those that filled the boats on the river, and from the great human belt that fringed the opposite shore, a cheer that seemed like tumult – it was a wild roar.

 Cork Examiner, June 1, 1911

WHITE STAR LINE.

TRIPLE-SCREW R.M.S. "OLYMPIC"
46,439 TONS.

Above *A White Star Line postcard of Olympic.*

JULY, 1908
Contract signed for construction of three new superliners.

MARCH 31, 1909
The keel is laid for ship number 401, the *Titanic*.

OCT 20, 1910
The first of the ships, *Olympic*, is launched.

MAY 31, 1911
At 12.15pm, the *Titanic* enters water for the first time.

JUNE 1911- MAR 1912
Hull fitted out. Masts, funnels and superstructure added.

OCT 1911
Titanic maiden voyage announced for April 1912.

Below *Titanic on the stocks at the Harland and Wolff shipyard in Belfast.*

arrangements of the 269-metre liner that were of greatest importance to the paying customers. Class was an overriding concern for society of the day. White Star, in common with other lines, divided its vessels into three classes to reflect these divisions. The cost of tickets on the *Titanic* varied hugely. A one-way ticket in a first-class suite could cost as much as £870 ($4350 or $50,000 at today's prices); a Second Class ticket was £12 (the equivalent of $60) and a third class ticket was just £7 ($40). The first and second classes were known as 'saloon' passengers, while third class became known as 'steerage' - perhaps because those who travelled in this way were occupying spaces used by 'steer' or cattle on other crossings. Despite the name, third class on the *Titanic* was said to be the equivalent of first class on some lines. But the higher classes enjoyed the upper part of the ship and more luxurious surroundings.

LIFE ON BOARD
Early claims about the *Titanic*, perhaps in part encouraged by the owners, suggested that it had a ballroom, a miniature golf course, a skating rink and even a theatre. None of these existed, but it did have a swimming

Deck over deck and apartment after apartment lent their deceitful aid to persuade us that instead of being on the sea we were still on terra firma. It is useless for me to attempt a description of the wonders of the saloon - the smoking room with its inlaid mother-of-pearl, the lounge with its green velvet and dull polished oak, the reading room with its marble fireplace and deep soft chairs and rich carpet of old rose hue - all these things have been told over and over again and only lose in the telling.

Southampton to Queenstown passenger William Browne, a trainee priest, from the Cork Constitution, April 13 1912.

pool, filled with tepid sea-water, a gymnasium, a squash court, smoking rooms and bars, libraries, a barbershop, a verandah café and various dining facilities. Passenger accommodation ranged from third class dormitories right up to self-contained apartments comprising bedrooms, sitting room and parlours, private baths, and even a private library, all en suite. Advance publicity pointed out that the *Titanic* was "as complete in her safety devices as in her luxurious outfit." The ship was divided into 30 compartments, separated by heavy bulkheads, or steel walls. It was believed that several of these compartments could flood without compromising safety, though there is no record that the White Star Line ever claimed it was "unsinkable."

FOOD ON THE *TITANIC*

Much of what was eaten in the ship's dining rooms would be unfamiliar today. Menus for all three passenger classes offered a great variety of options. Four meals a day were typical, even in third class. In the opulent surroundings of the first class dining room a staggering

Below *One of the grand staircases on board the Titanic.*

Above *A bronze cherub from the first-class staircase at the stern of the ship.*

Above *An artist's impression of a Second Class bedroom on the* Titanic.

eleven courses could be taken each night! A typical meal might start with oysters, washed down with a fine white Burgundy. A soup course came next, followed by a fish dish, a main course of beef or chicken, then a second main course which could be lamb with mint sauce, roast duckling with apple sauce, or sirloin of beef. A punch or sorbet came next to cleanse the palate, followed by small seventh, eighth and ninth courses of delicacies such as roast squab and cress, cold asparagus, and pâté de foie gras (made from the liver of a fattened goose). The choice of dessert included Waldorf pudding, chocolate and vanilla éclairs, French ice cream, and peaches in jelly. The eleventh course was an assortment of fresh fruits and mature cheese. Dinner concluded with tea or coffee, and waiters came round to offer the gentlemen their choice of cigar. An entirely different menu would be provided for guests the following night.

MARCH 25, 1912
Recruits sign up to crew ship. Men taken on in Southampton will be sent to Belfast.

MARCH 27
Captain Herbert Haddock in temporary charge. He will be replaced by Edward Smith.

APRIL 1
High winds cause sea trials to be postponed.

APRIL 2
Trials successful. Ship accepted by White Star. *Titanic* departs Belfast at night for Southampton.

APRIL 3
Spontaneous fire smoulders in a coal bunker close to the bows. Minor stokehold flood.

APRIL 4
Titanic berths at Ocean Dock in Southampton.

Titanic's "hotel" stock included 45,000 napkins, 50,000 towels, 18,000 sheets, 7,500 blankets, 5,000 table cloths, 800 eiderdown quilts; 12,000 knives and 12,000 forks, 19,000 spoons, 400 sugar basins, 400 cream jugs, 1,000 finger bowls, 12,000 cups and saucers, 1,200 teapots and 2,500 champagne glasses.

"The provisioning for one voyage alone tots up to such an onerous sum that few people would credit the figure if published, so that people are better left to their imaginations as to what it would cost to provide for three classes of travellers numbering in all about 3,100 souls, over an ocean journey of less than seven days out and the same time home, and provision for a crew of about 800 for one week in America."

Southampton Pictorial, March 18, 1912

Above *King Edward VII was on the throne at the time of the building and launching of the Titanic. Britain was still an industrial powerhouse and her shipbuilding skills second to none.*

he Titanic *had a largely trouble-free delivery journey to* Southampton, *the starting point of her maiden voyage to New York. Two incidents – a small fire and water entering a boiler room through a blocked pump – were not considered to be serious by the ship's crew. When it arrived, the* Titanic *had only a skeleton crew aboard, and one paying passenger from Belfast. The bulk of the crew would be taken on in Southampton.*

Below *A lifeboat nameplate from the Titanic, removed by a carpenter working on the Carpathia - the ship that was to later come to the stricken steamer's rescue.*

SAILING DAY

The *Titanic* spent a week at Southampton as it was prepared for its journey to New York. More than 6,000 tons of coal had to be collected from nearby ships because there was a national miners' strike that affected supplies. The ship was scrubbed throughout, and even its 70-foot funnels were cleaned. All the cargo that would be exported was brought on board. The number of crew on board reached more than 890, but one officer was reassigned elsewhere. His name was David Blair, and he took away a pair of binoculars he had previously lent to the lookouts. These were never replaced. The *Titanic* was ready to set sail on Wednesday April 10, 1912. Passengers had begun to board the ship by mid-morning. Pre-voyage checks by the Board of Trade were completed to ensure that the *Titanic* complied with safety and hygiene regulations were completed, and included the lowering of two lifeboats, mainly to see that they were seaworthy. They were swiftly hauled back aboard and made secure. The *Titanic* was required by company regulations to hold a boat drill on the voyage, to familiarise crew with lifeboat stations. It was not, however, a legal requirement. Boat drills were to be conducted by the crew after the

Fireman Joe Mulholland said that Thomas Andrews, the representative of builders Harland & Wolff came down to the stokehold on the trip to Southampton. He pointed to "insulting slogans about the Pope" which had been chalked up on the smoke-box... "He said: 'They are disgusting' and went off and returned with some sailors and had them removed."

Mulholland recalled that before *Titanic* set sail from Belfast, he took pity on a stray cat which was about to have kittens. At Southampton he was wondering whether to take a job as storekeeper for the Atlantic crossing when another seaman called him over and said: "Look Big Joe. There's your cat taking its kittens down the gang-plank." "That settled it. I went and got my bag and that's the last I saw of the *Titanic*."

 Sunday Independent, April 15, 1962.

MARINE LOSSES IN THE FIRST QUARTER (of 1912)

We give today a list of vessels that are considered to have been totally lost in March, together with the estimated values of ships and cargoes. The list includes 22 vessels and the total estimated value is £726,700 ($386,500). The losses are thus exceptionally severe. The corresponding table for January included 13 vessels of a total estimated value of nearly £600,000 ($319,100) and that for February contained 12 casualties, estimated to cost £382,000 ($203,200)... It seems likely that the winter of 1911-12 will take its place among the notoriously bad underwriting periods. The present year has started inauspiciously and should by any chance there be failure to salvage the bulk of the gold and silver in the *Oceana*, it would probably be easily the worst for underwriters that has ever been known.

The Times, April 2, 1912.

Titanic had left Southampton. Captain Smith had actually scheduled one to take place on Sunday morning, April 14 – the date his ship would strike an iceberg – but it was cancelled without explanation.

CROSSING TO CHERBOURG

The mighty *Titanic* was eased by tugs from its berth at Southampton to begin its journey to New York, stopping at Cherbourg, France, and Queenstown, southern Ireland, to pick up more passengers.

Left *The maiden voyage of the Titanic was to be 62 year old Captain Smith's last voyage before he retired.*

TIMELINE
10.04.12

8AM
First of the 'transatlantic' trains leaves Waterloo for Southampton.

9.30AM
Bruce Ismay, Managing Director of the White Star Line, inspects the ship with his wife and young children. He will remain aboard alone for the crossing.

11.50AM
A party of firemen leave the Grapes pub. A passing train prevents the Slade brothers from reaching the ship on time.

12.15PM
Titanic whistle blown three times to signal departure.

12.20PM
Near-collision with the drifting liner *New York*.

5.30PM
Titanic anchors between the port breakwaters at Cherbourg.

Below *A painting showing Titanic leaving Southampton on its journey to France.*

"My Dearest Bert... this is a tremendous boat. How I would love you to see it and explore it with me....

"I have my ring now and kiss it every little while and think of you. I will drop you a card as soon as I reach land. God bless you, and write me soon. With love, Annie."

Letter written written by third class passenger Mary Anne Perrault to her fiancé, Bert Pickett, April 10, 1912

"My Dearest Bert, no doubt you have heard about the terrible disaster. I am surprised to have landed safe. It was an awful experience, not soon to be forgotten. I have only the clothes I stand in - and my ring."

Letter from Mary Anne Perrault, dated April 18, written on the rescue ship Carpathia.
Eight months later, Mary Ann and Bert were married in Trenton, New Jersey. Chauffeur Bert had proposed
the day before sailing – April 9, 1912 – and given Mary Anne an engagement ring.

Above *Titanic was anchored at pier using its tremendously strong steel bollards, shown here being restored by engineers working for RMS Titanic, Inc.*

As the ship engaged its engines for the first time, the backwash from a propeller made the American liner *New York* pull against its moorings. The restraining ropes snapped and the New York was free. A collision with the *Titanic* looked inevitable, but prompt action by the tugs averted mishap and separated the vessels. Some onlookers saw it as a bad omen, while others were reminded of claims that the great size of the *Titanic's* sister ship had caused the British cruiser HMS *Hawke* to be drawn into a collision with the *Olympic* during September 1911. The excitement passed however. By about 1.30pm, the *Titanic* had moved into the Solent, an area of sea off the south coast of England, heading towards France. It arrived by early evening at Cherbourg, where 274 passengers were due to board the ship.

Those arriving by train from Paris included 142 first class passengers, most of them rich Americans. Among them were John Jacob Astor, reputedly the world's richest man, and his 19-year-old bride, Madeleine. Because the harbour at Cherbourg was not big enough for the *Titanic*, she anchored out to sea. A smaller ship, the *Nomadic*, was used to ferry out passengers and the mail that the gigantic liner was to carry across the Atlantic.

QUEENSTOWN: LAST SIGHT OF LAND

Shortly before noon on Thursday, the *Titanic* arrived on schedule at Queenstown, Ireland, where an excited crowd was gathered. The port was a busy place, handling around 30,000 emigrants a year. Ironically, on the day the latest wave of Irish people were preparing to leave their

Left *From Southampton, Titanic crossed to Cherbourg. The boat anchored a mile offshore so that the purpose-built tenders Nomadic and Traffic could bring more passengers on board.*

country behind forever, a third Home Rule Bill was being introduced to the House of Commons to give a measure of self-government to Ireland – legislation it was hoped might help stem the tide of emigration. To mark this new hope, Eugene Daly from Athlone played

Above The Titanic waits outside Queenstown, Ireland, to pick up more passengers.

the patriotic Irish air *A Nation Once Again* on his pipes as passengers boarded. Like Cherbourg, Queenstown did not have a dock large enough to handle the ship so the *Titanic* was anchored off Roche's Point, about two miles from the coast. Two boats ferried 123 mainly third class passengers to the ship, heading for what they hoped would be a new life in New York. More than 1,300 sacks of mail and 41 parcel

Left John Jacob Astor, said to be the world's richest man, boarded the Titanic with his pregnant wife, the 19-year-old Madeleine.

TIMELINE
11.04.12

6.45AM
Titanic passes Land's End, England, bound for Ireland.

9AM
Hours before *Titanic* is due to arrive, people assemble near Queenstown harbour to catch a glimpse of the latest triumph of ship construction.

12.15PM
Titanic drops anchor off the lighthouse at Roche's Point.

1.55PM
Anchor is weighed as *Titanic* leaves last European landfall.

2.15PM
British Army officer John Morrogh snaps the last photograph of the *Titanic*.

"This is a huge ship. Unless lots of people get on in Cherbourg and Queenstown they'll never half fill it. The dining-room is low-ceilinged but full of little tables for 2, 3 and more in secluded corners. How I wish someone I liked was on board, but then nice people do not sit at tables for two unless they're engaged or married. I wonder my blue blood didn't tell me that?

We nearly had a collision to start with. Coming out of Southampton we passed close to a ship that was tied up alongside the Oceanic, and the suction of our ship drew her out into the stream, and snapped the bonds that held her, and round she swung across our bows!

She had no steam up; so had to be pulled back by tugs, and we had to reverse. The name of her was the New York, in case you see it in the papers. It proves conclusively the case of the Hawke and Olympic."

Letter from First Class passenger Edward Pomeroy Colley to his cousin, April 10. Colley lost his life in the sinking, five days later, on his 37th birthday.

Above *The colourful Irish port of Queenstown.*

Right *A crewman watches as the Titanic prepares to leave Queenstown.*

hampers were also collected. The *Titanic* was not packed to capacity on her maiden voyage – third Class, for example, was less than two thirds full – and the White Star Line also made profits from the carriage of mail. Before the *Titanic* set off again, some of the lookouts began to question the ship's officers about the lack of binoculars, but the situation was never resolved. At 1.30pm the starboard anchor was raised for the last time and the *Titanic* departed on her first transatlantic crossing. Ironically, as the *Titanic* left Queenstown, the ship that was eventually to come to its rescue, the *Carpathia*, was setting off from New York.

LUCKY ESCAPES

For a handful of First Class passengers, the journey ended as they disembarked at Queenstown. Another lucky person, fireman John Coffey, hid himself under mailbags on a tender going ashore – and went home to his mother in Queenstown! Coffey lived to the age of 68. He died in 1957.

Right *Irish piper Eugene Daly treated his fellow passengers to an air on the pipes as the Titanic waited for extra passengers to be brought on board.*

Our Queenstown representative was one of the privileged few who had the honour of meeting Captain Smith on the upper deck of the *Titanic* on Thursday last, just outside his apartment underneath the elevated bridge of this massive steamer, previous to his departure from Queenstown.

I warmly complimented the veteran commander on his promotion to the largest steamship in the world. Captain Smith...quietly remarked that he fully realised his responsible position in having the command of such a luxurious ship with her immense number of passengers.

As he paced the deck of his noble vessel getting everything in readiness for his westward passage, he presented a fine appearance, clad as he was in his commander's blue uniform, but with a well-trimmed beard and standing six feet in height, he made a lasting impression on your correspondent. Shaking my hand warmly, he bade goodbye and sent his kind regards to friends on shore.

 Cork Free Press, April 18, 1912.

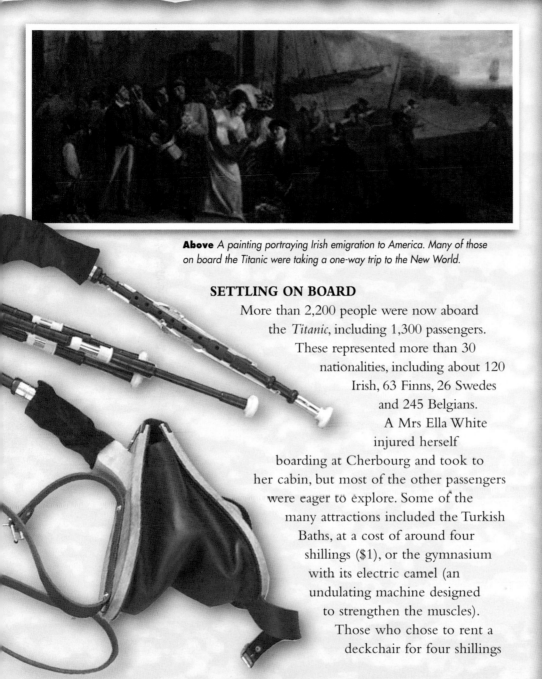

Above *A painting portraying Irish emigration to America. Many of those on board the Titanic were taking a one-way trip to the New World.*

SETTLING ON BOARD

More than 2,200 people were now aboard the *Titanic*, including 1,300 passengers. These represented more than 30 nationalities, including about 120 Irish, 63 Finns, 26 Swedes and 245 Belgians.

A Mrs Ella White injured herself boarding at Cherbourg and took to her cabin, but most of the other passengers were eager to explore. Some of the many attractions included the Turkish Baths, at a cost of around four shillings ($1), or the gymnasium with its electric camel (an undulating machine designed to strengthen the muscles). Those who chose to rent a deckchair for four shillings

TIMELINE
12.04.12

9AM
Crew lifeboat assignment lists posted. Most do not read them.

10AM
The captain leads his officers in a thorough inspection of ship.

NOON
The *Titanic* has made 386 miles since leaving Queenstown.

7PM
Titanic receives warning from *La Touraine* about two thick ice fields ahead.

11PM
Titanic's wireless apparatus breaks down.

Above *Over a thousand sacks of mail were brought on board the Titanic in Ireland.*

The desertion of stoker John Coffey made the news in light of *Titanic's* fate. The Cork Examiner reported that he had *"a lucky escape"* from being among those lost on *Titanic.*" It said that on the passage to Queenstown he had *"decided to get out of her, as he did not relish his job."*

A fellow fireman, survivor John Podesta, later recalled: *"Coffey said to me, 'Jack, I'm going down to this tender to see my mother.' He asked me if anyone was looking and I said no, and bade him good luck. A few seconds later, he was gone!"*

Other newspaper reports later claimed Coffey left because he *"felt sure something was going to happen."* Three days later, he joined the crew of the Cunard Line's *Mauretania* during her call at Queenstown. Family lore says he told New Yorkers on arriving that he had had a dream of the *Titanic* sinking, so left the ship.

Above *This set of playing cards was recovered from the wreck of the Titanic and is now part of an exhibition in Memphis, Tennessee.*

for the voyage were continuously passed by those taking the air on the promenade deck.

SOCIAL ACTIVITIES

So stately was the mighty ship that few below deck had any sense of being at sea. More than once, passengers were heard to remark: "You would never imagine you were on a ship." A lively social life had sprung up almost immediately on board the *Titanic*, structured around the class system. Second class passenger Lawrence Beesley, a British school teacher, looked down fondly from second class at

steerage passengers towards the stern who were engaged in an "uproarious skipping game." There was grander music in first class. A bugler summoned patrons to dinner with a few bars from *The Roast Beef of Old England.* After dinner, dozens sat in the beautiful first class lounge listening to the White Star orchestra playing from the *Tales of Hoffman* or *Cavalleria Rusticana.*

THE WIRELESS SYSTEM

For those feeling homesick, there was the option of sending a Marconi Wireless Telegram, at a cost of 12 shillings and sixpence (about $4) for the first 10 words. However, the system also provided valuable information about conditions at sea to the crew of the *Titanic*, so that when the wireless apparatus suddenly packed up during Friday evening it was cause for considerable concern. Captain Smith and his crew were relieved when it was repaired and working again by the early hours of Saturday. No-one was aware at this stage how much they would soon depend on it for their lives.

The rapid extension of the use of wireless telegraphy is shown by some figures in a report presented to the Conference (on wireless telegraphy at sea) by the German delegation. It appears that in the last four years, the number of ships, excluding warships, equipped with wireless telegraphy has increased from 52 to 926, and that during the same period the number of coast stations from 14 to 155.

 The Times, June 13, 1912.

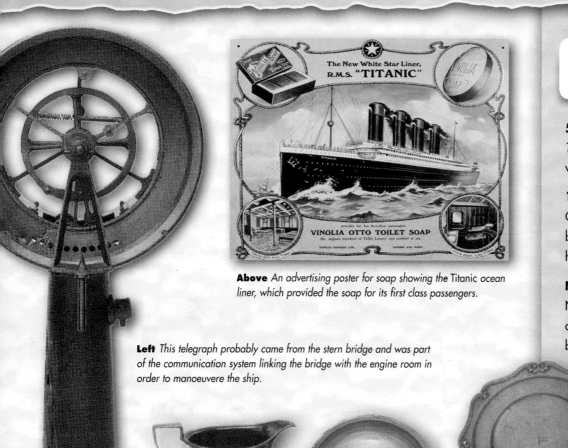

Above An advertising poster for soap showing the Titanic ocean liner, which provided the soap for its first class passengers.

Left This telegraph probably came from the stern bridge and was part of the communication system linking the bridge with the engine room in order to manoeuvere the ship.

TIMELINE
13.04.12

5AM
Titanic's wireless back in working order.

10.30AM
Captain Smith informed that the bunker fire in boiler room six has finally been extinguished.

NOON
Notices posted show that a distance of 519 miles has been covered since Friday.

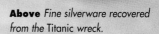

Above Fine silverware recovered from the Titanic wreck.

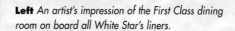

Left An artist's impression of the First Class dining room on board all White Star's liners.

Our Boulogne correspondent writes that one of the last vessels to sight the *Titanic* was probably the Boulogne steamer trawler *Alsace*...The trawler appears to have been rather dangerously near to the Titanic, passing so close in fact that she was splashed with spray from the *Titanic's* bow. The fishermen cheered the liner, and their salutations were responded to by the officer on the bridge.

The Times, April 22, 1912.

Above *After blundering into a giant iceberg, Titanic carried on for a few more minutes before the crew realised there was a problem.*

Below *Captain Smith grew increasingly worried about the fate of the Titanic after she had struck ice.*

The atmosphere on board the Titanic *during Sunday morning was calm and relaxed. Despite receiving a number of ice warnings, the crew seemed unconcerned, and a planned inspection of the lifeboats was scrapped by Captain Smith without explanation. Amazingly it was not a legal requirement for the crew to carry out these inspections, nor was it required for passengers to be assigned to lifeboats. By the end of the day, when the Titanic ran into a giant iceberg, this lack of planning would only add to the chaos.*

ICE AHEAD

Ice warnings had started to come into the *Titanic's* communication room during Sunday morning. At 9am, an ice warning was received from the ship *Caronia*, and was posted in the chart room by Officer Lightoller.

At 11.40am the Dutch liner *Noordam* sent a message warning of "much ice" in the same location. Further ice warnings were received from the White Star Liner *Baltic* and a German liner called *Amerika*. Captain Smith passed the first message on to Bruce Ismay, his managing director, who did not hand it back to him until the evening. In the early evening, a message was received from the *Californian*, just 50 miles to the north-west of the *Titanic*, and delivered to the bridge. This message warned of having seen three big

"We had smooth seas, clear, starlit nights, fresh favouring winds; nothing to mar our pleasure. On Saturday, as Mr Douglas and I were walking forward, we saw a seaman taking the temperature of the water. The deck seemed so high above the sea I was interested to know if the tiny pail could reach it. There was quite a breeze, and although the pail was weighted, it did not. This I watched from the open window of the covered deck. Drawing up the pail, the seaman filled it with water from the stand pipe, placed the thermometer in it, and went with it to the officer in charge."

- American first class passenger Mahala Douglas. Water temperatures were taken every two hours as a guide to changing currents and conditions.

Above *Captain Smith spent the afternoon in a first class suite like the one above with the Widener family.*

Left *The White Star Line's Managing Director, Bruce Ismay.*

icebergs in the vicinity. Captain Smith however was not notified of the danger because he was attending a party held in his honour by the rich American Widener family. Up on the bridge, officers were expecting to meet loose ice some time after 9pm. Smith visited the

9AM
The *Titanic* receives warning from the *Caronia* of bergs, growlers and field ice in her track.

11.30AM
Scheduled boat drill is cancelled.

NOON
Titanic has run 546 miles in the last 24 hours.

1.30PM
Second class purser Reginald Barker tells passenger Lawrence Beesley that the ship's speed is a disappointment.

11PM APPROX
Titanic is informed by the *Californian*, 35 miles to the north-west, that she is stopped and "surrounded by ice." The White Star liner rebuffs the message.

11.40PM
Titanic, travelling at 22 knots, grazes an iceberg on her starboard side.

"Just at that time I happened to be right in front of the crow's nest. My mate was telephoning, and I was standing in the front of the nest watching the berg.

It was higher than the forecastle; but I could not say what height was clear of the water. It was a dark mass that came through that haze and there was no white appearing until it was just close alongside the ship, and that was just a fringe at the top.

One side of it seemed to be black, and the other side seemed to be white. When I had a look at it going astern, it appeared to be white. She hit us. Close up against the side of the ship on the starboard bow.

The ship seemed to heel slightly over to port as she struck the berg. Very slightly over to port, as she struck along the starboard side."

- **Titanic** *lookout Reginald Lee in evidence to the British Inquiry.*

Left *There is no evidence that Captain Smith had been drinking the night the Titanic struck ice.*

Above *The ship's wheel, which has lain rusting at the bottom of the ocean for over 90 years.*

ignored this warning, telling Evans to "shut up" because he was "busy". At 11.40pm, lookouts Fred Fleet and Reg Lee were suddenly confronted with a dark object. The telephone rang on the bridge: "Iceberg, dead ahead!" First Officer William Murdoch had already spotted the obstacle. He yelled orders to reverse engines and to put the wheel hard-over to one side. The *Titanic* seemed to be inching towards escape before it plunged into the iceberg,

bridge at around 9.20pm and asked to be notified if the weather changed. Tragically, an advice message from the *Mesaba* warning of a "great number of large icebergs" directly ahead never reached the *Titanic*. Then just after 11pm, the *Titanic's* wireless operator, Jack Phillips, had another conversation with Cyril Evans, the wireless operator of the *Californian*. Evans said his ship was "surrounded by ice", but Phillips

accompanied by the screeching sound of buckling metal. Captain Smith ordered the engines to be stopped in order to inspect damage. Carpenter John Maxwell sent below to inspect (and possibly repair) any damage reported back that the ship was filling up with water – and fast.

CALLING FOR HELP

Captain Smith sent for shipbuilder and chief design engineer Thomas Andrews. Discovering that the ship was letting in water through the bow section and at least three other compartments, Andrews told Captain Smith that the ship had probably less than 90 minutes

"The Captain came in to the operating room. He told us that we had better get assistance. When Mr Phillips (Jack Phillips, senior operator) heard him, he came out (of the room where he had retired to sleep])and asked if he wanted him to use a distress call.

He said, 'Yes; at once.' The message was sent immediately. CQD about half a dozen times; MGY half a dozen times (CQD is a recognised distress call; MGY the code call of the Titanic).

I could read what Mr Phillips was sending, but I could not get the answers because he had the telephones. He told me to go to the Captain and report the *Frankfurt*. He was in communication with the *Frankfurt* and had our position.

I delivered that message to the Captain. He wanted to know where she was, her latitude and longitude. I told him we would get that as soon as we could."

- précis of the US Inquiry evidence of wireless operator Harold Bride.

 A ship's position is marked by the intersection of latitude (position between north and south) and longitude (position between east and west).

Above *A scene from the film Titanic (1997), showing how quickly the ship filled up with water after impact.*

Left *A telephone from the after docking bridge. It would have been used to send messages to the engine room or the navigating bridge.*

left before it sank. There were 2,200 people on board, but the 20 emergency craft on board the *Titanic* could carry only around 1,200 people. It was now 12.10am. Captain Smith fired out a chain of orders: all lifeboats were to be urgently cleared away. All crew were to be turned out and all passengers brought up on deck. Women and children were to board the lifeboats first. Everyone had to put on a lifebelt, while an emergency distress message was transmitted in order to summon all available assistance before the ship sank. The message, sent by wireless operators Jack Phillips and Harold Bride read – "CQD, MGY:41.46 N 50.14 W. We have struck a berg. Require assistance. Putting the women off in boats."

"My wife and I were awakened by the shock to the vessel. Listening a moment, I became aware that the engines had been stopped, and shortly afterwards hearing hurried footsteps on the ship deck, directly over our stateroom, I concluded that I would go out and enquire what had occurred. Partially dressing I slipped out of our room into the forward companionway, there to find possibly half a dozen men, all speculating as to what had happened. While we stood there an officer passed by somewhat hurriedly, and I asked him what was the trouble; he replied that he thought something had gone wrong with the propeller, but that it was nothing serious.

Leaving the few passengers that I had observed still laughing and chatting, I returned to my stateroom. My wife, being somewhat uneasy, desired to arise and dress. I informed my wife what the officer had told me. I decided, nevertheless, to again go out and investigate further."

- First class passenger Dr Washington Dodge of San Francisco.

TIMELINE 15.04.03

12.15AM
Titanic sends first distress message, giving an estimated position of Latitude 41.46 N, Longitude 50.24 W.

12.25AM
Ship's position corrected to 41.46 N. 50.14 W. CQD call from *Titanic* received by *Carpathia* says: "Come at once. We have struck a berg."

12.26AM
Fires drawn from the boilers to cool them before contact with water. Steam noisily blown out of the funnels.

12.30AM
Titanic to *Frankfurt*: "Tell your Captain to come to our help. We are on the ice."

12.35AM
Approaching ship's lights are seen. The order is given for rockets to be fired.

12.45AM
First lifeboat, number 7 on the starboard side, launched.

Above *This wrench was one of the tools used by the engineers who worked hard to keep the pumps and lights working.*

Above Artist's impression of the ship sinking beneath the water.

Even when they realised that the Titanic had been struck by an iceberg, many passengers were reluctant to leave the ship. Some believed the myth that had grown up around the ship, that it was unsinkable – while others were justifiably terrified of being cast out on the dark and freezing sea in basic lifeboats. This hesitation meant that valuable time was wasted and many of the ship's lifeboats went away half-filled. When another ship seemed to be approaching in the distance, persuading passengers to leave became even more difficult.

Above An artist's impression of the lowering of Titanic's lifeboats into the sea.

A LOST SAVIOUR

While the *Titanic* continued to fill up with water, a ship sighted in the distance offered a measure of comfort to those on board. Norwegian passenger Olaus Abelseth, 26, looked at the light from the port side, and could see it plainly. "A little while later there was one of the officers who came and said to be quiet, there was a ship coming." Captain Smith desperately ordered the crew in lifeboat 8 to row to the mystery ship to make her return with them to the *Titanic*. Fourth officer Boxhall fired rockets to attract attention. He was joined by two quartermasters, and rockets were fired, yet the ship refused to continue towards the *Titanic*. A misguided hope that the mystery ship might rescue the *Titanic*, coupled with a reluctance to leave the ship, meant that many of the spaces on the *Titanic's* lifeboats were not taken up. The first lifeboat lowered, Boat 7, had room for 65 people, yet just 28 people boarded. Boat 5 was lowered into the sea with 24 spaces left unfilled. Boat 1 left with just 12 of its 40 places filled. Boat 8 fared better, and 39 out of its 65 spaces were filled. Lifeboat 4 left with room for 25 more people on board. Both collapsibles were swept away and saved only boarders.

DEATH OF A MAIDEN

Back on board the *Titanic*, the news reaching Captain Smith was increasingly bleak. There was no hope of containing the flooding: it had already filled the first two boiler rooms forward along with steerage accommodation in the bows,

"As one of the lifeboats was being filled with women and children, a foreigner tried to jump in the boat. The officer told him to go on deck. He refused, and the officer fired, and the man fell dead on deck. The crowd of foreigners who were hanging around the lifeboat cowed back when they found one of their countrymen dead.

"The lifeboat was lowered, and the officer kept on firing his revolver until he was level with the water. I saw a similar instance occur on the port side. A passenger tried to claim a seat in one of the boats. The officer told him to leave at once, and as he hesitated a revolver shot was fired, and he dropped dead in the water."

 - Steward C. W. Fitzpatrick, quoted in the Northern Constitution, May 4, 1912.

Above Titanic's hull was badly damaged by the crash. The ship sank in just over two hours.

the post office and the squash court. Because the bulkheads only went up as high as D–deck, the water overflowed at the top, rushing down palatial corridors into new sections of the vessel. It tumbled downstairs into areas that had previously been dry. At 1.20pm the engineers called off their efforts to delay the inevitable and

Above Lifejackets were provided to passengers on the Titanic but they did little to protect people from the freezing temperature of the North Sea.

12.55AM
Lifeboats 6 and 5 launched on opposite sides of Titanic.

1AM
Lifeboat 3 launched. Crewmen still "all standing about," according to fireman Alfred Shiers who left in 3. "They did not think it was serious."

1.10AM
Lifeboat 8 told to row for the light on the port side. Lifeboat 1 departs from the starboard side with only twelve occupants.

1.25 AM
Olympic asks her sister ship: "Are you steering southerly to meet us?" *Titanic* replies: "We are putting the women off in boats."

"My attention until the time I left the ship was mostly taken up with firing off distress rockets and trying to signal a steamer that was almost ahead of us.

I saw his masthead lights and I saw his side light. By the way she was heading she seemed to be meeting us, coming toward us."

US Inquiry chairman Senator William Smith: "Do you know anything about what boat that was?" - "No, sir."

"Have you had any information since about it?" – "None whatever."

"You say you fired these rockets and otherwise attempted to signal her?"

"Yes, sir. She got close enough, as I thought, to read our electric Morse signal, and I signalled to her; I told her to come at once, we were sinking."

"I told the Captain about this ship, and he was with me most of the time when we were signalling. I went over and started the Morse signal. He said, 'Tell him to come at once, we are sinking.'"

- **précis evidence of Fourth Officer Boxhall to the US Inquiry.**

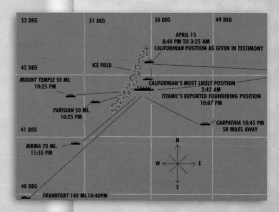

Above Map pinpointing the exact position the Titanic found itself in trouble, and the distance of the nearest ships to the stricken vessel.

Above *A gold wristwatch found in the First Class section of the boat. More First Class passengers made it to safety than any other passengers.*

Below *Captain Arthur Henry Rostron of the Cunarder Mauretania, in his uniform as aide De Camp to the King of England.*

abandoned the pumps. They were ordered up top, and told to equip themselves with lifebelts. It is a myth that the engineers remained at their posts until they were swallowed by the sea. By now, complacency was replaced by terror on deck. The *Titanic* was visibly slumping in the water. Departed lifeboats failed to respond to megaphone calls that they return to the side of the ship to take on more. The panic led to gunshots to stop rushes at the remaining boats. No-one admitted to seeing killings at the Inquiries, but some witnesses were quoted in the press. Finally, the boats were all gone, and the *Titanic* was no more.

RESCUE AND RETURN

It was after 4am when the Cunard liner *Carpathia*, responding to the SOS, reached the *Titanic*. The first lifeboat the *Carpathia* found was Boat 2. It contained Fourth Officer Joseph Boxhall, who confirmed to the *Carpathia's* Captain, Arthur Rostron, that the *Titanic* had sunk at 2.20am. Meanwhile exhausted survivors were being hauled up on board. Rostron cancelled his voyage and decided to head for New York with some 712 survivors. Questions were being asked even before the *Carpathia* arrived in New York. How could a major liner make such a long journey with so few lifeboats? Why were there so many empty places in the lifeboats when they were finally launched? And why was the *Titanic* going so fast at night in reported ice? In the absence of many firm facts, the waiting press engaged in speculation and sensationalism. It was inferred from the

"Captain Rostron, the commander of the Cunard Liner *Carpathia* was today presented with a cheque for ten thousand dollars, raised by public subscription by the New York American.

Acknowledging the cheque, Captain Rostron declared that he would never forget the way in which he had been received by Americans, though he again maintained that the members of his crew were entitled to equal credit. "I shall use this cheque," he said, "for the education of my three sons, whom I hope to bring up as worthy representatives of the Anglo-Saxon race."

New York World, June 4, 1912.

"Captain Smith stood next to me as we got in (to lifeboat 8), and told Tom Jones, a sailor who acted nobly, to row straight for those ship lights over there, land the passengers aboard, and return as soon as possible.

"For three hours we pulled steadily for the lights seen three miles away; then we saw a port light vanish and the masthead lights grow dimmer until they disappeared."

 - Nöelle, Countess of Rothes, interview in the Journal of Commerce, April 1912.

known lists of survivors that first class men behaved nobly by giving up their lives and lifeboat places for the 'weaker sex' and defenceless children. From there it was a short leap to conclude that steerage passengers had behaved in a hysterical, cowardly fashion, jeopardising lifeboats through their panic. The inference was that the better class of people must have fended them off, and that the crew had been obliged to shoot. By the time the *Carpathia* arrived, rumours had established the notions that the band had played the hymn *Nearer, My God, to Thee* as the ship sank, or that cowards had escaped dressed in women's clothing.

WHO WAS TO BLAME?

Official investigations into the circumstances surrounding the sinking of the *Titanic* were carried out first by the US Senate, and then by the British Board of Trade. The investigations arrived at very different conclusions. In the United States, the mood towards the crew was hostile,

Above *The mystery of exactly how the ship sank was not solved until the 1980s.*

TIMELINE 15.04.12

1.45AM
Last signals from *Titanic* heard by the *Carpathia*, rushing to the rescue but still hours away. "Engine room full up to boilers."

1.50AM
Lifeboats 2,9,10,11,12,13,14, 15 and 16 have all left. Only five boats remain.

1.55AM
Lifeboat 4 is launched. Captain Smith tells wireless officers that they have done their full duty.

2AM
White Star Line MD Bruce Ismay leaves in collapsible boat C. Hundreds, including women and children, remain.

2.05AM
Collapsible boat D leaves. Other passengers attempt to free boats A and B from the roof of the officer quarters.

2.20AM
Boat A is swept off, waterlogged; boat B capsized by waves. *Titanic* sinks.

"The disproportion between the numbers of the passengers saved in the first, second, and third classes is due to various causes, among which the difference in the position of their quarters and the fact that many of the third class passengers were foreigners, are perhaps the most important.

The disproportion was certainly not due to any discrimination by the officers or crew in assisting the passengers to the boats. The disproportion between the numbers of the passengers and crew saved is due to the fact that the crew, for the most part, all attended to their duties to the last, and until all the boats were gone."

Proportions saved:	1st class passengers 203 out of 325, or 62.46 per cent.
2nd class	118 out of 285, or 41.40 per cent.
3rd class	178 out of 706, or 25.21 per cent.
Crew	212 out of 885, or 23.95 per cent.

Total on board saved 711 out of 2,201, or 32.30 per cent.

British Inquiry final report, July, 1912.

Above *The Titanic was equipped with enough boats to rescue 53 per cent of those on board, but only 32 per cent were saved. The boat above was one of the few that left filled.*

Top *Cover of a newspaper running an account of the sinking of the Titanic.*

Below *Mr. and Mrs. Bruce Ismay arrive at the Court following the Titanic disaster. Mr. Saunderson, General Manager of the White Star Line, is shown on the left.*

with the *New York Herald* lamenting that "so many American lives were wasted by the incompetency of British seamen." Forty-three crew members were detained in New York and ordered to give evidence at the Senate Inquiry. The Senate held Captain Smith fully responsible for taking the *Titanic* at such speeds in such treacherous conditions. The British Inquiry however decided that speeding in the vicinity of ice did not amount to reckless navigation, after hearing evidence that it was common practice among liners seeking to meet tight schedules. The court ruled that the tragedy had provided a warning – and that similar behaviour in light of what had happened would constitute negligence. More controversially, both the US and British Inquiries concluded that the lights seen by the sinking *Titanic* had belonged to the 6,200-ton freighter *Californian*. This vessel had seen rockets, undoubtedly from the *Titanic*, but her officers had been unsure of what they signified. They were "low-lying," yet they linked them to another ship a few miles away. In reality the *Californian* had been on track to Boston, more than 20 miles to the north.

REFORMS

Original plans for the *Titanic* showed 48 lifeboats, but in the end it provided only 20. This was actually more than the number of lifeboats required by Government regulations. The regulations were inadequate because they had not been changed since 1894, when the largest vessel on the water was less than a quarter of the *Titanic's* size. After the tragedy the law was changed to ensure there was lifeboat capacity for everyone on board, and all ships at sea were compelled by law to monitor their wirelesses continuously for any distress signals. All ships carrying more than 100 passengers were also required to have a watertight inner hull. History suggests that the lessons of the *Titanic* were quickly learned. Just ten days after it sank, coal stokers on board its sister ship the *Olympic* went on strike because there were not enough

Above *Mrs Navratil journeyed to New York and was reunited with her children, who had featured in newspapers all over the world.*

lifeboats on board, and the voyage was cancelled. The strikers were arrested. When *Titanic's* second sister ship, *Britannic*, struck a mine just two years later on September 21, 1916, it sank in approximately 55 minutes, but this time only 30 people lost their lives. A further legacy of the *Titanic* disaster was the establishment of an International Ice Patrol that continues to this day.

One of the most romantic mysteries of the Titanic tragedy is that of two little waifs, aged four and two years, who were rescued from the wreck. Miss Margaret Hays, a young woman of wealth and culture, took the children to the beautiful home of her father, where they were cared for. Now the mystery is solved. The names of the children are Michel and Edmond Navratil, of Nice, and their pet names are Lolo and Momon. Their father, with whom they were travelling to America on board the *Titanic*, married 17-year-old Marcelle Collata. Two lovely boys were born to them, but petty disagreements arose and a year ago they agreed to separate. The father got possession of the boys and started with them for America under the assumed named of Hoffman. When the *Titanic's* lifeboats were being filled, he came forward and placed his sons in one, but stepped back and went down with the ship.

**Christian Herald,
June 5, 1912.**

TIMELINE
16-22 April 1912

APRIL 16
Early British newspaper editions claim *Titanic* is being towed to Halifax, Nova Scotia, Canada.

APRIL 17
Carpathia makes it clear that it is the sole carrier of survivors.

APRIL 18
Rescue vessel arrives in New York at night in a thunderstorm.

APRIL 19
First sitting of the US Senate Inquiry. Bruce Ismay is the first witness.

APRIL 20
Wireless operator Harold Bride says in evidence that the *Titanic* was repeatedly warned of ice.

APRIL 21
Search ships *Minia* and *Mackay-Bennett* arrive in vicinity of bodies from the wreck.

APRIL 22
Evidence shows that Marconi tried to gain a publicity advantage from the tragedy.

Above *A birdseye view of the crowds as they wait outside the White Star Line office, awaiting news of the Titanic disaster.*

"We knew nothing until the Carpathia docked, and all sorts of weird rumours were afloat as she came to her pier. One was that she was bringing about 300 dead; another was of panic and shooting while filling the lifeboats.

As soon as the passengers got off the Carpathia and the survivors began to come ashore, a large number of them made a bee-line to the various newspaper offices to tell the story of the wreck and how they were rescued - fixing their price first. Some of them had photos too. As you know, the fact that J. Bruce Ismay came safely to shore while a lot of his passengers were left to drown caused a lot of talk.

Hearst's papers have been full of vituperation and abuse for him, printing his name in large type under his picture ' J. Brute Ismay.' They also had a cartoon of him in a lifeboat full of women, looking like a poor shivering coward."

New York Herald staffer J. Norman Lynd in a letter, April 1912.

Above *Papers published tales of heroic engineers such as Arthur Ward who worked on as the ship sank.*

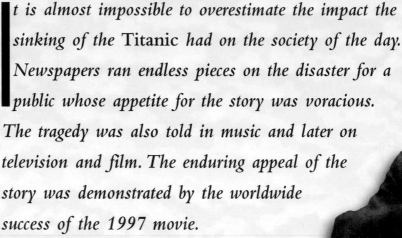

*I*t is almost impossible to overestimate the impact the sinking of the **Titanic** had on the society of the day. Newspapers ran endless pieces on the disaster for a public whose appetite for the story was voracious. The tragedy was also told in music and later on television and film. The enduring appeal of the story was demonstrated by the worldwide success of the 1997 movie.

NEWSPAPERS

The press reflected various public moods, not least the national humiliation that quickly seized Britain after so appalling a loss. Myths were forged to make the reality more palatable – that the band nobly played hymns to the end, that the engineers remained at their posts until caught by torrents of water rushing in, and that the crew and men from first class behaved selflessly. No-one felt it was in bad taste to print what were described as 'thrilling' stories of the disaster. Newspapers ran campaigns to raise money for the widows and orphans left by the disaster. The press never quite let the story go, and in the 1950s and 1960s would still report the death of a survivor whom none of their readers had ever heard of.

THE DISASTER IN MUSIC

The first piano selections to "honour the dead" appeared within weeks of the *Titanic's* demise. Some had better titles – and melodies - than others. One record was entitled *Be British,* supposedly after the Captain's last words, while another bemoaned *The Ship That Will Never Return.*

Right *The sinking of the "unsinkable" Titanic continued to grab newspaper headlines across the world years after the event.*

A music sheet told how *My Sweetheart Went Down With the Ship*, complete with a picture of a couple staring into one another's eyes on a sloping deck. So much attention was attracted in France by the band playing the hymn *Nearer, my God, to Thee* as the *Titanic* went down that a speedy translation, *Plus près de toi, mon Dieu*, was published, and sold 50,000 copies in less than a week. One news agency reported that the hymn was so popular it was being sung by groups at street corners. In the United States, the sinking became the subject of songs known as negro spirituals. Although there were few black people aboard, the theme had a distinct appeal and led eventually to a popular campfire song, *It Was Sad When the Ship Went Down*. In late 1997, the signature song of the movie *Titanic*, My Heart Will Go On" by Celine Dion, became a massive worldwide smash. Ironically it helped to sow fresh interest in the actual music played on the Titanic and spin-off recordings flourished – winning new converts to classical music from the world of popular music.

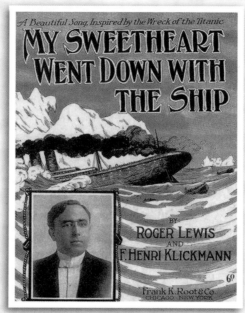

Above *The cover of a popular piece of sheet music - "My Sweetheart Went Down with the Ship."*

FILM AND TELEVISION

Movies were made almost immediately after the sinking of the *Titanic*. One dramatic treatment appeared on celluloid within a few weeks of the disaster, starring actress Dorothy Gibson, who had actually been a first Class passenger saved from the ship. The Great War served to push the story from the public mind, although it re-emerged in a 1929 movie, *Atlantic*, which the

MAY 15, 1912
Lord Mayor of London closes his *Titanic* fund as it reaches £262,000 ($140,000).

MAY 24, 1912
Titanic band tribute in London. Nearly 500 musicians, "the greatest professional orchestra ever assembled" play.

APRIL 15, 1913
Titanic memorial lighthouse opened in New York.

APRIL 29, 1914
Engineers' Memorial unveiled in Southampton.

JULY 29, 1914
Statue unveiled to Captain Smith in Lichfield, England.

JUNE 1920
Memorial unveiled in Belfast.

Left *Canadian singer Celine Dion had a worldwide hit with her theme from the film Titanic (1997).*

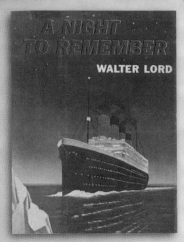

Above *The famous book* A Night to Remember *inspired a fresh interest in the*

White Star Line immediately denounced as a slur on British shipping. In 1938 the great film director Alfred Hitchcock announced plans for a feature production of the story, but World War II intervened, and with it came a German version of the disaster that portrayed the British on board as incompetent cowards. In 1955, Walter Lord's book *A Night to Remember* inspired a major revival of interest, and a film of the same name, starring Kenneth More as Second Officer Lightoller, followed to great

success a year later. The discovery of the wreck in 1985 led to new TV programmes, including one in which the actor Telly Savalas opened a recovered Titanic safe in a live broadcast to discover not jewels but a mass of sodden papers. In 1997 the James Cameron movie *Titanic* captured the public imagination once more. The set was half a replica ship built in Baja, Mexico, with the Pacific rather than the Atlantic, as the backdrop. More than three hours long, it starred British actress Kate Winslet and US heart-throb Leonardo DiCaprio and won 11 Oscars. It was the most successful motion picture of the last century and the first film to gross more than $1 billion worldwide. Viewers were so seduced by the love story that the inevitable collision broke the spell in a horrifying manner, and to great cinematic effect, thanks

"Some jump, some fall, each dotting the water's surface like the period at the end of a sentence. Then, the stern slips under the water, plunging everyone into a coldness so intense it is indistinguishable from fire. Ten minutes. Twenty minutes. The inchoate wail of fifteen hundred souls slowly fades to individual cries from the darkness. We know you can hear us! Save one life! Seven hundred survivors stand by in lifeboats built for twelve hundred, afraid to act for fear of getting swamped. They tell themselves that the voices from the water do not belong to their husbands or their loved ones. They are merely the cries of the damned…"

- From the screenplay to Titanic, directed by James Cameron for Paramount Pictures and Twentieth Century Fox. The movie became the highest-grossing of the last century, taking more than $1 billion at the box office. It had also been the most expensive movie ever made, at $200 million dollars.

"High in the crow's nest of the new White Star Liner Titanic, Lookout Frederick Fleet peered into a dazzling night. It was calm, clear and bitterly cold. There was no moon, but the cloudless sky blazed with stars. The Atlantic was like polished plate glass; people later said they had never seen it so smooth.

This was the fifth night of the Titanic's maiden voyage to New York, and it was already clear that she was not only the largest but also the most glamorous ship in the world. Even the passengers' dogs were glamorous."

The opening lines of the classic Titanic book A Night to Remember, by Walter Lord. The book prompted a whole new generation to begin researching the Titanic — ironically, as they did so, discovering that the book they had regarded as their Bible was littered with mistakes.

Above *The lifeboats are lowered in a scene from the 1997 film* Titanic.

TIMELINE
1928-1934

1928
Sinking of the *Vestris*, and every other peacetime tragedy at sea, causes the Press to invoke the *Titanic* as the worst of all.

1931
Captain Arthur Rostron, rescuer of *Titanic* survivors, publishes memoirs titled *Home From the Sea*.

A lifebelt marked S.S. *Titanic* is reported washed up in May on the shore of Gravesend Bay, New York.

1934
A troubled White Star Line merges with its rival, Cunard, to become the Cunard White Star Line.

to computer-generated animations. Spin-offs included 3-D movies on the state of the wreck, a documentary on the director's visit to the site, and the 3-D movie, DVD and coffee table book *Ghosts of the Abyss* (2003).

TITANIC ON CANVAS

From the moment that construction of the great ship began, it inspired those interested in the visual arts. As well as the photographs taken for postcards and for the shipyard's own publicity, it was also painted by artists working for the White Star Line. A canvas painted in 1912 by the acclaimed maritime artist Charles Dixon, *Titanic Being Fitted Out at Queen's Island, Belfast,* hangs in the Ulster Folk and Transport Museum. Since then, the ship has been painted by a host of amateur and professional artists, none with more realistic detail than the modern American artist Ken Marschall, whose additional paintings of how the wreck looks today are justly famous.

TITANIC ON THE STAGE

Theatrical drama about the ship is much more scarce. The ship had a cameo in the play Cavalcade by the famous author Noël Coward, later turned into a movie in 1932. Various musicals and other adaptations came and went, many being panned by the critics for even attempting to make entertainment out of such a difficult subject. But the stage musical *Titanic* was a smash hit on Broadway just before the close of the 20th Century. A number of minor playwrights have mined dramatic material from the various Inquiries, including the Texan author Pat Cook, and Belfast-based Denis MacNeice, whose play *Blackness After Midnight* focuses on the 'trial' of Captain Lord of the *Californian*.

Below *The tale of the sunken supership has even reached the stage. Here, some of the cast from the stage musical* Titanic *wait to board the ship.*

Left *Plans for a Titanic film directed by the master of suspense Alfred Hitchcock vanished with the outbreak of war.*

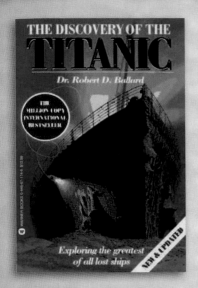

THE DISCOVERY OF THE
TITANIC
Dr. Robert D. Ballard

THE MILLION-COPY INTERNATIONAL BESTSELLER

Exploring the greatest
of all lost ships

NEW & UPDATED

Above Dr Robert Ballard, discoverer of
the Titanic wreck, wrote a popular book
about his work.

After the Titanic *was sunk, and the last survivors had been hauled to safety, the grim task of recovering and burying the dead began. Today, graves for the ship's dead can be found all across the world. The search for the largest victim, the ship itself, began almost immediately after the disaster. It would be more than 75 years, however, before its remains were discovered.*

IDENTIFYING THE DEAD

In 1912 it was left to four little ships to seek out the floating bodies of those who were lost. Fewer than 330 victims were recovered by the *Mackay-Bennett*, *Minia*, *Montmagny* and *Algerine*.

A significant number were reburied at sea after identification. Others lie in three cemeteries at the Canadian home port of the search vessels. In Halifax, Nova Scotia, a large plot includes the stone of obscure Irish trimmer marked J. Dawson. This marker was festooned with flowers in the wake of the 1997 movie *Titanic* by those who believed it was the actual grave of Jack Dawson, the character played by Leonardo DiCaprio. *Titanic* steward William Cheverton's body was discovered by the steamer *Ilford* on June 8, 1912, and

THE DEATH SHIP AT HALIFAX
A Gruesome Spectacle

The *Mackay-Bennett* reached port this morning and discharged her freight of 190 bodies, landing her sad burden occupying the whole day. Bodies lay in a great pyramid of coffins on deck, while others, uncoffined, were piled under tarpaulins. The latter were the first to be removed.

When the coverings were first thrown back more than fifty bodies were disclosed to sight. They lay on their backs with the sunlight shining into their sightless eyes. Some bore an appearance of repose, but the features of others were contorted. Men with stretchers were quickly engaged in the work of removal...the bodies were then taken in charge by the undertakers.

These quickly placed the bodies in rough pine boxes and lifted them into black hearses which hastened off at the rate of one a minute.

Many of the bodies were without clothing. According to the *Mackay-Bennett's* crew, none of the bodies bore bullet marks.

- **Press Association despatch from Halifax, Nova Scotia, April 30, 1912.**

Centre *On Thursday, April 17, the ship Mackay-Bennett steamed to the site of the Titanic's sinking to search for bodies. The first corpses were brought aboard on April 21.*

Above *Work crews exhume the remains of three unknown victims of the infamous Titanic shipwreck, in Halifax, Nova Scotia, May 17, 2001.*

buried at sea. His body was the last to be recovered. More recently, science has been used to try to identify some of the unidentified victims of the tragedy. DNA testing in this century has revealed that the "unknown child" buried by crewmen of the *Mackay-Bennett* in Halifax in 1912 was Eino Panula, a 13-month-old Finnish boy.

SEARCHING FOR THE WRECK

Expeditionary voyages to find the *Titanic* had been planned almost as soon as the ship sank. One firm contracted with a number of bereaved families in 1912 to locate the wreck, raise it, and recover their loved ones' remains. Predictably nothing came of it. In 1913, there was an organised "pilgrimage" by some widows to the spot where it was believed the *Titanic* sank, and flowers were scattered on the waves. Over the years, there have been many strange

1935
Second Officer Lightoller pens his account, *Titanic and Other Ships.*

1939
Hitchcock movie *Titanic,* slated to begin shooting, is scrapped.

1953
First expedition to find the wreck mounted by salvage firm Risdon Beasley.

1962
Fiftieth anniversary marked. Death of Stanley Lord, whose *Californian* was wrongly identified as the nearby ship.

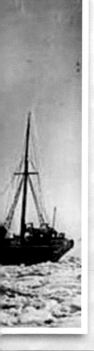

Right *Map showing the location of the wreck site*

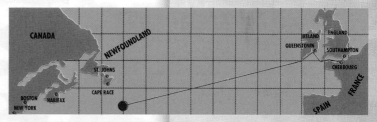

"About 12.30 on Tuesday we were playing shuffleboard on deck when we noticed our boat making a sharp turning movement. We could not make it out, and thought at first a derelict was in front, but after a few minutes we sighted the lifeboat in the water on our starboard (side).

We passed within 50 yards of it. By then our engines had been stopped, so we could plainly see the three men in it. It was the most pathetic sight I have ever witnessed. One man was lying under the bows and the other two in the stern. Their legs were under the thwarts, and this no doubt held them in the boat. They all had lifebelts on, and we could see their faces were almost black."

Letter from Harry Church of Birmingham, England, who was on the Oceanic on May 15, exactly a month after the tragedy, when it discovered the wallowing collapsible A lifeboat with abandoned bodies 350 miles from the scene of the sinking.

SEPT 1, 1985
A deep-towed sonar imaging system on Knorr research ship shows a giant boiler on ocean floor – the first sign the famous wreck has finally been found.

Above *A photograph of a chandelier from the Titanic beamed across the world.*

"I turned to Jean-Louis. The look in his eyes said everything. The *Titanic* had been found. We'd been right all along. Then he said softly, 'It was not luck. We earned it.'

Our hunt was almost over. Somewhere very near us lay the RMS *Titanic*…larger and larger pieces of wreckage were now passing under Argo and Earl had to winch in to avoid hitting them. We didn't yet know where the main wreckage was.

As the images on the video screen grew more and more vivid — large pieces of twisted hull plating, portholes, a piece of railing turned on its side — for the first time since I had started on this quest 12 years before, the full human impact of the *Titanic's* terrifying tragedy began to sink in.

Here at the bottom of the ocean lay not only the graveyard of a great ship, but the only fitting monument to the more than 1,500 people who had perished when she went down."

- Dr Robert D. Ballard, The Discovery of the Titanic, Madison Publishing, 1987.

schemes to find the *Titanic*. Many never went further than empty talk and idle dreams, but British salvage firm Risdon Beasley did mount a reconnaissance in the 1950s, while Texan oil millionaire Jack Grimm poured millions into abortive expeditions that came up empty-handed. In 1977, a British submarine encountered a sonar hit on a large wreck that may have been the *Titanic*. But in 1985 the search ended, when an French–American expedition found the exact spot of the wreck. Someone in the British military establishment tipped off the London *Observer* newspaper that the *Titanic* had been found and it became a front-page story. The story was fractionally ahead of the truth, but on the day it was printed – September 1, 1985 - the remains of the *RMS Titanic* came back into view for the first time in 73 years, thanks to underwater imaging equipment. It was found by a joint expedition led by Jean-Louis Michel and Dr Robert (Bob) Ballard, and funded by ocean science institutes in both countries. News of their success came while they were still at sea, and the world was electrified.

There were immediate calls to raise the *Titanic*, echoing the title of a popular novel and film. The discovery confirmed two things – that the ship had broken in two as it sank, contrary to the finding of the British Inquiry, and that it had not been where it said it was in its SOS transmissions, but more than 13 miles further east. This latter fact explained the failure to find it in earlier expeditions. It also confirmed the testimony from the *Californian* in 1912

Above *Dr Robert Ballard on board a research vessel in 2004.*

Left *A submersible is sent down to visit the site of the wreck.*

about where rockets had been seen. The British Inquiry had believed that the SOS position was accurate and that the *Californian* observers had been lying.

A CENTRE OF INTEREST

The wreck of the *Titanic*, 560 miles from Newfoundland, has been the focus of dozens of expeditions since. Tourist dives have been available to individuals at a cost of $20,000 a time, and many trips have been given away as prizes by radio stations and commercial interests. It is possible that this cheapening of the vessel's significance reached its lowest point – more than two miles down – when David Leibowitz and Kimberley Miller exchanged vows in a submersible and were officially married on the *Titanic*. Since the discovery of the wreck, a debate has been raging on the salvage question. Thousands of items have been retrieved from the "debris field", despite the objections of some survivors who pointed out that it is still a mass grave. Many of the items recovered are everyday – a tube of toothpaste, bottles of Bass ale – but they prove compelling enough to draw thousands to travelling exhibitions of recovered artefacts.

"The discovery of the *Titanic* and re-awakening of interest has had many effects, from world-record prices of £50,000 sterling (about $266,000) for a menu from the ship and $100,000 for a baggage tag, to the advent of some 120 new books.

One man claims to be the reincarnation of shipbuilder Thomas Andrews and has hindsight on the sinking. Another author insists there was no iceberg at all, and that the *Titanic* was ripped asunder in her keel by flat and low-lying ice.

One thing is sure: the *Titanic* will eventually be wholly re-imagined, since the wreck is succumbing ever more steadily to the ravages of time. A coat of 'rusticles,' created by iron-eating bacteria, covers the remnants of the hull. In time, she will be no more.

Court rulings have done little to protect the vessel, since she lies in international waters. The many visits by submersibles, landing on the bow, have hastened her demise and eventually another tragedy could result. Even two miles down, she is still as vulnerable as ever. "

Extract from a talk by **Titanic expert Senan Molony.**

PRESERVATION EFFORTS

The condition of some recovered items has been little short of wondrous. Leather pouches preserved papers from the worst ravages of seawater while they lay on the seabed for decades. But most artefacts had to undergo painstaking scientific conservation efforts. Two laboratories in France have restored hundreds of items including postcards, paper money and business cards using a

Above *David Leibowitz and Kimberley Miller scuba-diving. They later married on board the Titanic.*

Above *An underwater shot of the rusted bow of the Titanic.*

"On April 15, 1912, the world awoke to the news that the RMS *Titanic* had met with disaster off the coast of Newfoundland. And ever since that time, the misinterpretation of the evidence that was given at the Courts of Inquiry has perpetuated the myth that the Titanic collided with an iceberg."

- Blurb for the book The Sinking of the Titanic, The Mystery Solved by Captain L. M. Collins (2003). He suggests that the ship ran on to pack ice which tore its bottom. This may be partly accurate, but the airbrushing of the iceberg from history seems a touch extreme.

technique called electrolysis. In 2000, all the artefacts collected were taken to a laboratory in the United States owned by RMS Titanic, Inc.

SCIENCE OF THE *TITANIC*

The US company RMS Titanic was finally named salvor-in-possession of the shipwreck in 1994. The company carries out archaeological surveys and scientific analysis, working with the Center for Maritime and Underwater Resource Management (CMURM), experts in underwater archaeology. Microbiologist Roy Cullimore has carried out investigations into the deterioration of the wreck, and has discovered that up to 20 per cent of the bow of the *Titanic* has already been lost to corrosion. This has led to calls that advocate breaking into the wreck to retrieve items, before the hull collapses completely and buries them forever. It is estimated that this could happen in less than a century. RMS Titanic, Inc, has also used forensic engineers to look at why the vessel broke in two when it sank. They concluded that stresses in its mid-section caused the *Titanic* to bend and eventually buckle during the disaster. Studying the scatter of material on the seabed has also provided clues as to the phases of the breakup of the ship. Exciting work using sonar technology has also enabled the RMS Titanic to capture images of the damage caused by the iceberg that brought down the *Titanic*. The pictures taken show that, remarkably, the damage was not one great hole torn into the boat but a series of thin slits.

Above *A scientist holds a cherub statue recovered from the First Class aft staircase of the Titanic during a dive in 1987.*

Left *A robotic arms retrieves a leaded glass window from the shipwrecked Titanic in 1991.*

Below *A silk bow tie and other personal belongings from a suitcase retrieved from the seabed.*

2002
Identification of the "Unknown Child" from a bone fragment after the grave was controversially opened in May 2001.

2004
Titanic's foremast, which had been lying against the bridge, collapses into the forward well deck as rust deterioration steadily claims the ship.

2005
Three survivors still alive. Lillian Asplund, Barbara West and Millvina Dean were all toddlers or babies when the vessel sank.

2012
The 100th Anniversary. Plans are under way to re-create the exact maiden voyage, in the same places on the same dates, but this time minus the iceberg.

"A recently advanced theory claims that the *Titanic* was really lost because of a bunker fire. This hypothesis ranges from the implausible (a weakening of the steel from heat) to the incredible (that the iceberg was just a ruse to cover up a darker negligence of incompetent fire-fighting). No evidence is provided – or even a decent explanation of how a fire in a 15-foot-deep bunker could compromise a hull along a 250-foot impact zone. (But) simply mention the word 'cover-up' and all ears are riveted."

- Expert Bill Sauder, writing in the Titanic Commutator, official journal of the US-based Titanic Historical Society, Inc.

Above *Divers raising part of the hull to the surface.*

Although the fate of the **Titanic** was set from the moment it struck ice, the reactions of those on board played a crucial role in determining what would happen next. The crew of the ship acted in a number of different ways - some heroic, some less so. Those fortunate enough to survive provided the British and American Inquiries into the disaster with valuable accounts of what happened as the ship went down, as did those passengers who escaped with their lives.

EDWARD JOHN SMITH, Captain

Edward John Smith was born on January 27, 1850 in Staffordshire, England. He began to study for a career on the seas in 1871, and joined the White Star Line in 1880. Smith was given his first command just seven years later. During the Boer War Smith commanded several troopships, building on a fine reputation. He became Commodore of the White Star fleet in 1904. Smith took charge of the *Titanic* and joined her maiden voyage as he did for all White Star's newest ships. Despite his fine reputation, Smith seemed to act in an indecisive way after the *Titanic* struck the iceberg, and he died on board the ship. His body has never been found. The British Inquiry cleared Captain Smith of negligence although it considered the *Titanic* had been travelling at "excessive speed", but the US Senate found Smith at fault for the tragedy.

WILLIAM MURDOCH, First Officer

William Murdoch was born on February 28, 1873 in Dalbeattie, Scotland. After serving on many sailing vessels, he eventually went on to join the White Star Line. Murdoch was the officer on watch who tried to avoid the iceberg. An experienced mariner, he also played a leading role in ensuring a disciplined evacuation for the starboard lifeboats. Murdoch fired shots to clear men out of lifeboats and accounts at the Inquiries testify to his bravery. He died during the tragedy and his body was never found.

CHARLES LIGHTOLLER, Second Officer

Charles Lightoller was born in Lancashire, England, on March 30, 1874. He began his career at sea at the age of just 13. In 1898 Lightoller spent a brief spell as a cowboy in Atlanta, United States, but returned to the sea to join the White Star Line in 1900. Lightoller helped rescue many passengers during the sinking of the *Titanic*, and was the most senior surviving officer. In 1940, at the age of 66, Lightoller took a ship called the *Sundowner* to rescue soldiers from the beaches at Dunkirk during World War. He died on December 8, 1952, having retired from the Navy just six years earlier.

HERBERT JOHN PITMAN, Third Officer

Herbert John Pitman was born on November 20, 1877, in Somerset, England. At the age of 18, he joined the Merchant Navy, and went on to qualify as a Master Mariner. In 1906 he joined the White Star Line. He was on board the *Titanic* for her sea trials, and for the voyage itself. Pitman's duties included determining the ships position, deck supervision and standing watch on the bridge. At the hearings in the United States and Great Britain, Pitman recorded that there were no lifeboat drills. During the disaster, Pitman helped with the uncovering and launching of several of the lifeboats, and escaped himself to the safety of the *Carpathia*. Pitman later served on the *Titanic's* sister ships the *Olympic* and the *Oceanic*, and also went on to serve during World War II. Pitman died on December 7, 1961.

BRUCE ISMAY, Managing Director

(Joseph) Bruce Ismay was born on December 2, 1862 near Liverpool, England. He was the son of a founder of the White Star Line. Ismay took charge of the firm when his father died in 1899. In 1901, he began negotiations which saw the company become part of the American company International Mercantile Marine (IMM). Ismay regularly boarded the maiden voyages of his ships, and so was on board as a first class passenger for the *Titanic's* first (and last) trip. Bruce Ismay left in one of the last boats, and was heavily criticised by the press for saving himself while so many of his passengers died. Ismay retired the year after the sinking, unable to carry on in the face of such criticism. He lived quietly, often at his Irish fishing retreat, until his death in 1937.

ARCHIBALD GRACIE, U.S. passenger

Colonel Archibald Gracie was born on January 17, 1859, in Alabama, United States. He was a member of the rich Gracie family, but became wealthy in his own right through property. He eventually became a colonel in the United States Army. Gracie boarded the *Titanic* at Southampton as a First Class passenger. Gracie was one of those who survived on Collapsible B. He tried unsuccessfully to revive a lifeless passenger in the boat. Gracie went on to write a book, *The Truth About The Titanic*, but he never fully recovered from the sinking of the *Titanic*, and died on December 4, 1912, before his book was published and before he had even finished proofing it. Many of the *Titanic's* survivors attended Gracie's funeral at Woodlawn Cemetery, New York, together with members of his regiment.

LAWRENCE BEESLEY, British passenger

Second class passenger Lawrence Beesley was born on December 31, 1877 in Derbyshire, England. A keen scholar and Cambridge graduate, in 1904 Beesley became Science Master at Dulwich College, England. Beesley boarded the *Titanic* at Southampton as a second class passenger, paying £12 for his ticket. Saved in lucky lifeboat 13, Beesley and his fellow occupants endured a moment of terror as it seemed lifeboat 15 would fall on top of them. After his dramatic rescue, Beesley was inspired like other survivors to write a book about the disaster, *The Loss of the SS Titanic*. He also attended the filming of the movie *A Night to Remember*, where he actually tried to stay on the ship as the sinking was being filmed. Beesley died on February 14, 1967 at the age of 89.

COLONEL JOHN JACOB ASTOR, First Class passenger

Colonel John Jacob Astor IV was born in New York on July 13, 1864. Educated at Harvard, he was an inventor, writer and businessman. In the 1890s, Astor built some of New York's finest hotels, including the Waldorf-Astoria. During the Spanish-American war, he became lieutenant colonel in the US volunteers. Astor married for the first time in 1891, but created a stir in 1909 when he divorced to marry eighteen-year-old Madeleine Force. After spending time abroad to escape the gossip, in the spring of 1912, Astor and his new wife decided to return to the United States on the *Titanic*. When the ship struck ice, Astor remained unconcerned, and was reluctant to leave *Titanic* for a lifeboat. He stayed on board while his wife was loaded into a lifeboat, and lost his life in the disaster. Madeleine Astor died on March 27, 1940.

SENATOR WILLIAM SMITH, Chairman, US Inquiry

Born on May 12, 1859, in Michigan, United States, Senator WIlliam Smith spent the beginning of his working life practising law. He then served as a Republican senator from 1895-1907. Smith was ignorant of maritime matters, but persuaded President Taft to allow him to hold an inquiry as soon as the survivors landed. Officers and crew, including company head Bruce Ismay, were served with subpoenas when they arrived. Smith's Inquiry yielded much interesting information, despite his occasional apparent stupidity. He once asked what an iceberg was made of. "Ice", came the reply, through gritted teeth. Smith was very interested in finding out the name of the Mystery Ship seen when *Titanic* was sinking. The Inquiry infuriated the British who regarded their flagged ship as none of America's business.

ARTHUR ROSTRON, Carpathia Captain

Captain Arthur Rostron was born on May 14, 1869 in Lancashire, England. At the age of just 13 he joined a Merchant Navy training ship and set out to sea. Roston went on to join the Cunard Line in 1895, and to command many of the Line's great ships, leaving briefly to serve in the British Navy during the Russo-Japanese War. On April 11, 1912, he guided the *Carpathia* out of New York towards Europe. It was on this journey that the ship would come to the aid of the *Titanic*. Rostron would win the Congressional Medal of Honour for his role in rescuing so many of the *Titanic's* passengers. He preferred to praise his crew and wireless operator, who caught the distress message while supposedly unlacing his boots just before going to bed. Rostron died on November 4, 1940.

ROBERT HICHENS, Quartermaster

Robert Hichens was born on September 16, 1882, in Cornwall, England. By 1906 he had reached the level of Master Mariner, and served on many vessels around the world. At the wheel when *Titanic* struck, Hichens later found himself in charge of Lifeboat 6, surrounded by women. He had no crew, so the women had to row. Several later complained about his coarseness and doubts they could survive, and complained that he ignored requests to row back to collect more passengers, and the matter was raised at both the British and American Inquiries. Hichens went on to serve on other boats, but towards the end of 1933 he shot a man over a debt and was sent to jail. He was released in 1937, and died on September 23 1940 aboard the cargo ship *English Trader* during World War II.

LORD MERSEY, British Inquiry President

John Charles Bigham was born on August 3, 1840 in Liverpool. He worked as a barrister and judge, and when he retired in 1910, he was made Lord Mersey. Lord Mersey was chosen by the British Government to chair the investigation as to why there had been such heavy loss of life on the *Titanic*. Mersey presided over what Officer Lightoller later described as a "whitewash," clearing the Board of Trade, responsible for shipping, of any failures. Lord Mersey turned in a report with the officially-desired conclusion that the accident could not have been anticipated. His obituary in the London Times in 1929 was unusually sour, saying Mersey "did not possess the higher intellectual gifts," was "too apt to take short cuts, and by no means free from the judicial fault of premature expression of opinion or bias."

GLOSSARY

Aft the "after" part, behind a ship's "forward" area.

Amidships in the middle of the ship.

Annihilate to reduce to nothing.

Astern towards the stern, or rear of a ship.

Augur to promise or act as a sign for the future.

Bosun's chair a canvas cradle on a rope.

Bows the leading knife-edge of a vessel.

Berth place for a ship to tie up.

Blueprints architectural drawings.

Bridge control room of a ship.

Bulkheads metal walls to create compartments.

Capsized turned over.

Celluloid movie film on which pictures are recorded.

Cliché a phrase made tired and worn by over-use.

Commissioned ordered.

Commodore senior Captain among Captains.

Compartments contained areas.

Complacency the assumption that there is nothing to worry about.

CQD "Come Quickly Danger", a forerunner of SOS.

Cutters smaller lifeboats.

Debris field area of scattered wreckage.

Disembark to leave ship.

DNA Deoxyribonucleic acid, genetic information that is unique to each individual.

Epitome essence or summary.

Equator an imaginary circle round the earth, at an equal distance from the north and south poles.

Fathom a measure of depth, 1.82 metres.

Fore the front or towards the front.

Forecastle (also known as foc'sle because of the way it is pronounced) the front part of a ship, usually crew quarters.

Freighter a ship that carries only or mostly cargo.

Funnel a passage for the escape of smoke, especially on a ship.

Gangway door opening in a ship's side.

Gantry a platform or bridge for a travelling crane, used in construction of ships.

Growlers low-lying, small icebergs.

Hard-a-starboard throwing the ship's wheel fully to the right.

Home Rule proposal to give a regional parliament to Ireland.

Hull the whole of a ship's outer plating.

Immigrants persons entering a country. Those leaving a country are emigrants.

Inchoate incomplete, only begun, undeveloped.

Infer to assume from given information.

Insatiable cannot be satisfied.

Jeopardise to endanger.

Keel a ship's lowest part or bottom.

Knot one nautical mile per hour.

Latitude a way of measuring distance from the equator using angles.

Longitude the arc (curve) of the equator expressed in degrees east and west.

Lucrative valuable, financially rewarding.

Mandatory required by law.

Memoirs personal recollections in written form.

Memorabilia items associated with a person or event, for remembrance.

Modifications changes.

Moorings restraining ropes.

Morse a simple code devised by Samuel Morse, using dots and dashes for letters of the alphabet. It is used in telegraphy or by flashing signal lights.

Muster summoning, assembly.

Myriad a great many.

Navigation carrying out an intended ship's course.

Obituary newspaper review of a life to mark someone's death.

Oceanographic relating to ocean research.

Onerous burdensome.

Pillory to heavily criticise or denigrate.

Poop The poop deck was at the stern.

Port the left side of a ship.

Promenade to walk or take the air.

Reappraisal reassessment.

Redemption saving, recovery.

Reincarnation the rebirth of someone who has lived before.

Rivets steel nails used to attach plating.

Rusticles like icicles, name given to formations of rust.

Salvage to recover what can be saved.

Scapegoat a person given all the blame for an incident.

Shuffleboard a deck game that uses a puck and numbered squares.

Side light a light shown on ships, green on the starboard side and red on the port side.

Solent body of water between Southampton and Isle of Wight.

Sonar echo-location apparatus.

SOS the distress message "Save Our Souls".

Starboard the right side of a ship.

Stateroom passenger cabin.

Steerage another name for third class.

Stern the rear part of a ship.

Stringent demanding, strict.

Submersible a craft capable of going underwater.

Subpoena a legal compulsion, "under penalty" if not complied with.

Superstructure the deck buildings on a ship.

Tarpaulins heavy waterproof coverings.

Thwarts the planks across a small boat for seating.

Turkish baths a way of cleaning the body using steam rather than water.

Vainglorious with excessive pomp and show.

Vexed angry, annoyed.

Vituperation abuse and name-calling.

Vortex whirlpool.

Wallowing lying low in water.

Weigh anchor raise the anchor

Well deck a sunken deck between superstructures.

Wireless telegraphy sending out Morse code by radio waves.

INDEX

ACKNOWLEDGEMENTS

PICTURE CREDITS:

Every effort has been made to trace the copyright holders, and we apologize in advance for any unintentional ommissions. We would be pleased to insert the appropriate acknowledgements in any subsequent edition of this publication.

B=bottom; C=centre; L=left; R=right; T=top

Alamy: 4-5c, 10b, 18t, 24t. Corbis: 1, 9b, 14-15c, 21t, 28b, 29t, 35t, 36b, 37t, 37b, 38-30 all. Everett Collection: 2, 7b, 23t, 32-33c, 33t, Getty Images: 8l, 13b, 30c. National Maritime Museum: 6b, 10c, 14cl, 18b, 21tc, 22 all, 23b, 25c. Senan Molony: 16b, 20b, 24cl, 29b, 30tl, 31t, 34t, 36tl, 40-43 all.